WHERE HAVE ALL THE CORPORATE BUYERS OF VETERINARY PRACTICES COME FROM?

How your Exit Strategy Attracts Highly - Qualified
Buyers Paying Top Dollar for Your
Practice So You Can Transition on Your Terms

by Joseph Hruban

*Find out how to best position yourself and your practice for your
eventual exit at:*

www.DVM-Transitions.com

ISBN-13: 978-1985616127
ISBN-10: 1985616122

WHY DID I WRITE THIS BOOK?

I wrote this book because of my work as a consultative broker and advisor, assisting doctors in the transition from active practice to the next chapter in their lives. Practice owners need information and guidance as they navigate through the uncharted waters encountered along their individual exit paths.

It is not that I have all the answers for the senior DVM; rather, by asking questions, I can help the practice owner make better-informed decisions in line with their personal values and needs.

Depending on the unique characteristics of the doctor's personality, objectives, and hospital or clinic, each exit strategy will be different.

Given that many DVMs are receiving solicitations from non-operator owner/investors, it became increasingly apparent that the practitioner needs a resource to help them make better decisions in an arena with which they are not accustomed. It is in this spirit that this book was written.

> # Free Bonus
> # Complimentary Snapshot Valuation
>
> Having a general idea as to what your hospital or clinic might be worth to a buyer is a good first step to take in your planning. Then take steps to improve.
>
> www.DVM-Transitions.com/bonus

TABLE OF CONTENTS

Chapter 1

THE BIG PICTURE

"Compound interest is the eighth wonder of the world. He who understands it, earns it ..... he who doesn't ..... pays it."

– Albert Einstein

While corporate interests have long been investing in veterinary practices, recently the trend has accelerated significantly as larger and more varied types of buyers enter the market for owning veterinary practices.

Where have the corporate investors come from, and what are the dynamics of the changes upon the practice of veterinary medicine in this country, and on the lives of individual veterinary practitioners as they transition from owners to employees and/or into retirement?

Before we attempt to fully explore the current buying phenomenon, let's set the stage just a bit......

You are busy and don't have time to research and analyze the market.

If you're a veterinarian, you're likely very busy in your practice and probably don't have time to research and analyze the current state of the veterinary transition market, let alone the ongoing changes. You'd probably like to have a better understanding of the current situation and evolving changes, and it's likely most DVMs feel the same way.

Many factors are out of anyone's control, per se, because after all, as the saying goes, "The market's going to do what the market's going to do." As business people we have to react and adjust to these changes.

Going to a conference out of town, sleeping in a strange bed, hearing lots of new ideas and meeting new people can help provide a much-needed "pattern interrupt" in your thinking. This also helps you create the time and opportunity to consider the changes happening in our industry, and helps you develop ideas about how you can deal with these changes.

Ultimately, the more we know, the better we can potentially position ourselves for things and events which will impact us, and will probably continue to do so at an ever-increasing rate of change.

Therefore, the objectives here are to review the landscape, make some observations, and see how we might be able to better position ourselves to take action both near-term as well into the reasonably foreseeable future.

So first of all, we want to know where we're at today. What are the factors that contribute to the current environment for buying and selling veterinary practices?

One of the driving factors in the business landscape throughout the world right now is an extremely low interest rate environment, including countries with zero interest rates, and indeed, even negative interest rates in some countries. Never before in the history of the world have we seen such low interest rates being set by the central banks of so many countries.

This ultra-low rate environment is really a remnant from the worldwide 2008-2009 financial debacle, when the balance sheets of banks were shattered, and the only way that the resulting economic pain and potential further disaster could be mitigated was to make the cost of capital equal to zero. That way lenders could re-engage in lending, or at least in buying low-yielding Treasuries for, in essence, "free money" and a risk-free return on capital.

In due time, these measures allowed the banks to rebuild the equity within their balance sheets and ultimately recover from the debacle. Even though the banks were responsible for their bad behavior they were deemed "too big to fail and too big to jail." And ultimately the bailout was and always will be shouldered by the taxpayers.

In Europe today there are countries with negative interest rates. That may sound, and is mind-boggling, and indeed, never before in the history of interest rate policy have central banks driven rates first to zero and now below zero.

Negative rates penalize savers and anyone who needs to derive income from interest-paying investments. And on top of getting virtually no yield, participants in this market still need to deal with some rate of inflation; depending on what they purchase, true inflation varies. Consumers who have certain expenses such as health care, and higher education, have costs increasing at rates far above the average cost of living, costing users of those services disproportionately much higher than the government's "Consumer Price Index" of 2.5%.

19 European Countries with Negative Interest Rates

COUNTRY	% YIELD
Switzerland	-0.92 %
Czech Republic	-0.81
Germany	-0.74
Netherlands	-0.71
Sweden	-0.70
Denmark	-0.69
Finland	-0.67
Austria	-0.65
Ireland	-0.58
Belgium	-0.57
Slovakia	-0.57
France	-0.53
Slovenia	-0.38
Spain	-0.37
Bulgaria	-0.33
Italy	-0.17
Portugal	-0.08
Cyprus	-0.08
Lithuania	-0.08

Data as of August 2017

As of this writing, third quarter of 2017, there are 19 countries, all in Europe, that have negative interest rates.

These dynamics pose a quandary for investors, who need to get a yield or at least some kind of return on their money, while outpacing inflation. Otherwise their real rate of return is negative.

Take the 10-year Treasury Bond, for example, currently yielding about 2.5%. Now let's say a DVM is selling their practice for $1 million, and would like a risk-free return on that money. Investing the $1 million in the 10-year Treasury Bond yields 2.5%, representing only $25,000 per year. That's not going to "move the needle" in terms of a retired doctor's lifestyle. In the past, when the comparable rate was 7%, the retiree would receive $70,000 annually. That's quite a difference.

Let's look a little deeper into the history of rates. Over the last 50 years, the average 30-year home mortgage carried a rate of 8% (yes, hard to believe by today's standards).

Average 30 Year Mortgage = 8%
(for period April 1971 thru December 2017)

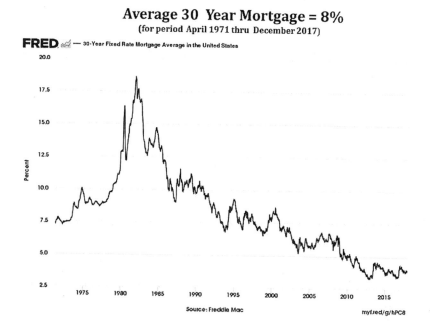

FRED — 30-Year Fixed Rate Mortgage Average in the United States

Source: Freddie Mac   myf.red/g/hPC8

Years ago, when pension plans made their actuarial commitments and projected their long-term forecasts for beneficiaries, they assumed there would be a 7.5% or so long-term rate of return. While those numbers existed years ago, fast forward to today.

Pension plans can only get 2.5 % risk free returns today, and they're committed to actuarial forecasts of 7.5 %. This poses a major problem, because now they have a huge projected shortfall. And that in turn places immense pressure on investment managers (and investors generally) to engage in "chasing yield."

Investors Reaching for Yield:
10-Year US Treasury Bond Rates (Jan 1962 - Dec 2017)

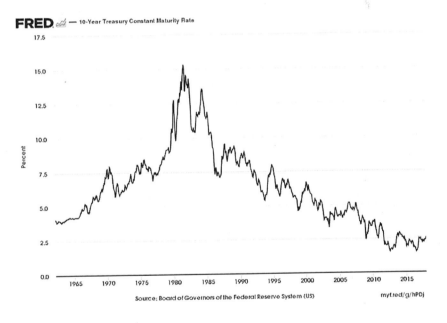

"Chasing yield" simply means buying investments that carry more risk than you might otherwise be willing to take, solely because lower-risk investments don't provide enough yield to provide the returns necessary to satisfy investment objectives. "Chasing yield" also implies the investor is unaware or ignoring the additional risks embedded in this process.

So right now, there are few safe places for institutional investors, such as banks, insurance companies, pension plans, and large pools of money being managed for other people.

This poses the question: What would YOU do if you were a professional investment manager? How would you position the capital under your management?

Ultimately, all investment managers seek a return on investment. They seek to do so with the least amount of risk consistent with their needs to achieve a specified rate of return.

Thus, in the current landscape, with interest rates so low, they have few viable alternatives. But they do need to achieve asset growth on some level, and if they don't grow, they risk failure. We're seeing that today, with the outlook being that many of the pension plans around the country may not be able to provide the benefits promised. And of course, this includes the Social Security program, though technically it is not a pension plan, nor was it designed to be a retirement plan.

One of the alternatives to lower yielding bonds that investment managers might pursue is the stock market, primarily a growth-oriented universe of publicly held companies, which in turn, either have to grow, or they will not attract capital, and will be neglected or sold off by the investment community.

How do companies grow? They can grow organically from within, from ongoing product development, marketing and business activities, and customers referring other customers. That is called organic growth. You see it within your practice.

Typically with publicly held companies organic growth only goes so far, and when a company reaches a certain size (varying widely by industry) in order to continue their growth path the company will seek to accelerate growth through making acquisitions, or perhaps by merging with other companies.

The quickest way to grow is to go out and purchase other companies through mergers and acquisitions.

This then is why we are in a situation where certain investors have "discovered" the veterinary community, which is perceived as providing a stable rate of growth in excess of the inflation rate, which is viewed as quite attractive. In addition, these investors see the industry as somewhat "recession proof" as people continue in tough times to seek medical care for their pets, as was observed during the last recession.

The veterinary practice as an investment opportunity has been discovered. Bottom line: basically, people with pools of money need to invest, and corporations need to grow. These dynamics will continue to shape the future of veterinary care across the country. Now is a good time to take an assessment of where you stand businesswise and determine how these changes might affect your practice and transition plans.

Chapter 2

CASH FLOW

"I'm a cash flow guy. If it doesn't make me money today, forget about it."

– Robert Kiyosaki

The U.S. economy has grown at less than a 3% annual rate for a record straight 12 years. This is as measured by Gross Domestic Product, commonly known as GDP, which simply stated represents the total value of everything (all goods and services) produced by all people and companies within a given country in one year.

Just as it's harder for companies to continue high growth rates as they mature, as a national economy ages over the decades it is similarly challenging to continue a high growth rate.

Intuitively, industries which are growing faster than our economy would seem to be interesting to investors. Such is the case with the veterinary space. Since it has been growing at a compound annual rate of 4.9% (vs. 3% for the economy as a whole) the veterinary opportunity is very attractive to

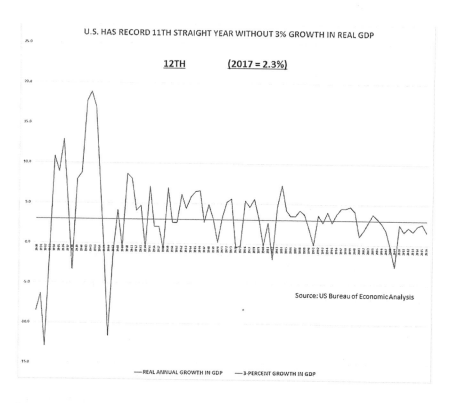

U.S. HAS RECORD 11TH STRAIGHT YEAR WITHOUT 3% GROWTH IN REAL GDP

12TH   (2017 = 2.3%)

Source: US Bureau of Economic Analysis

——REAL ANNUAL GROWTH IN GDP   ——3-PERCENT GROWTH IN GDP

investors. Percentage- wise 4.9% is 163% greater than 3% so the 1.9% differential is much larger than it might sound at first blush.

And, when you look at the fact that in 2016 almost $67 billion was spent on our pets in the U.S., with about 25% of that going to veterinary care, well that's an attractive niche opportunity for investors.

In addition to the high relative growth of the industry, investors are attracted by the stability of that growth. Our own intuition, supported by studies, shows that in the last economic downturn, people continued caring for, and spending on, their pets, (And animals have generally been viewed by most as a very satisfying emotional investment, perhaps even more so in difficult times.)

So it's no wonder, according to dvm360, that corporate investors and other consolidators are lining up looking for opportunities to come into the marketplace.

About 3,000 of the approximately 26,000 veterinary hospitals in the U.S. are owned by corporate investors. It is likely that many if not most of the remaining 23,000 hospitals are underperforming on some level, thus they can be viewed as ripe for improvement with corporate management. It's easy to see why there is so much corporate interest in veterinary opportunities today.

With the exception of venture capitalists seeking high risk growth opportunities, or bargain-seeking vultures trying to buy severely undervalued assets, savvy investors focus on cash flow. Cash flow is the lifeblood, the oxygen of all business activity.

Investors have established methodical ways to analyze cash flow, so that they can compare and contrast (apples to apples) different investment alternatives. So, to standardize the cash flow that they can really analyze, they apply several basic steps to the numbers as presented on a company's income statement.

Here's the gist of it. They start with the reported taxable income, add back taxes paid, add back the interest expense, add back any depreciation taken, and they also add back amortization.

Cash Flow ...... EBITDA

- **E**arnings
- **B**efore
- **I**nterest
- **T**axes
- **D**epreciation
- **A**mortization

Let's examine each of these in some detail.

Why add back interest expense? Interest is added back to taxable income because the cost of capital will be different for every investor, and it is unlikely the new investor will have the same borrowing costs, so in essence, the current owner's interest expense is not relevant to the new buyer's decision.

Similarly, the prospective buyer will adjust the income for any income taxes paid, because they will likely have a different tax rate than the current owner.

The new investor will then add back any depreciation shown on the income statement, primarily because it is a non-cash item, and they're trying to look at adjusted cash flow. You don't have to write a check for depreciation, because you already wrote that check when you bought the asset that you're depreciating.

In addition, amortization is added back. You can think of amortization as depreciation for intangible assets. For example, a trademark might be amortized for its expense over the useful life of the trademark. Similarly, when you purchase a practice you are paying for goodwill. Goodwill is an intangible asset which will be amortized over a period of time.

So, the prospective investor will adjust the cash flow for these items, and they use an acronym: **EBITDA** which stands for Earnings Before Interest Taxes Depreciation and Amortization.

So that's the mystery of EBITDA, explained. Whenever you hear something that sounds like "Eeh-Bit-Duh"or "Eh-Bid-Dah" that person is referring to the acronym EBITDA" just think of it as an approximation for the actual operating cash flow of the business. It's a formula for the cash flow that the new buyer would anticipate receiving if they were the owner of the business, and it the most widely used criteria for business valuation comparison purposes.

Nearly every business person does just about everything reasonable (some more so!) to minimize taxes.

To quote Judge Learned Hand, "Any one may so arrange his affairs that his taxes shall be as low as possible; he is not bound to choose that pattern which will best pay the Treasury; there is not even a patriotic duty to increase one's taxes."

So the private business person should and hopefully will deduct every legitimate expense that they can in order to minimize taxes.

However, when it comes time to sell a business, it just might be a prudent planning step to consider letting more go to the bottom line by trimming unnecessary discretionary expenses such as that $10,000 continuing education trip to Hawaii. Consider taking that CE locally, let that $10,000 go to your bottom line, thereby beefing up net income.

Yes, in this scenario you will pay more in taxes in the short run, but since tax rates are a fraction of 100%, there will be higher net cash flow which will be viewed favorably by prospective buyers. This is true whether the buyer is your associate or a corporate investor. Your associate will likely be funded by a lender for 100% of the purchase price. The lender will want to see strong cash flow. And you will get a better price as a seller.

Remember, cash flow rules the day. Focus on your bottom line as you approach your exit. Where you have discretionary expenses you don't have to take, then take your foot off the expense pedal.

Going back to EBITDA, according to the 2016 AVMA Report on Veterinary Markets, the average for all practices across the country, in terms of EBITDA, is 14% of gross revenue.

Also, if 14% EBITDA is the average for all practices throughout the country, then what do the top performing practices generate? According to the AVMA, the top 20% of all veterinary practices generate on average 25% EBITDA, a very attractive level.

If you can imagine an investor spending a million dollars for a practice, and they're getting $250,000 off that investment per year, that's plenty of cash flow to pay interest. To pay taxes. And to pay themselves a healthy return far greater than an economy that's growing at under 3% annually.

So take a look at your add-backs, and see where your EBITDA stands.

If that's not something you're comfortable doing, I'd be happy to help you out. Just shoot me an email and I'll make the calculation for you.

Chapter 3

CORPORATE DEALS COMPLETED

To paraphrase Warren Buffett, he says one of the best businesses in the world is a toll bridge, because all you do is maintain the bridge, people drive over it, and they give you money. It's pure cash flow.

He's got a good point. So, on the subject of cash flow and EBITDA, how can a practice that might be average in terms of its cash flow make improvements to get above average? We need to look at certain benchmarks to see where the expenses are.

The average practice spends about 46% of its top line revenue on labor and benefits. No shocker there.

However, what do practices that are performing in the top 20% of all veterinary practices spend on labor and benefits? According to the AVMA, it is about 40%. That's a 6-point percentage differential between the average and the top group.

2014 EXPENSES

	Top 20%	All Practices
Direct Costs	20%	22%
Labor & Benefits	40%	46%
Other Expenses	15%	18%
EBITDA	25%	14%

2016 AVMA REPORT on VETERINARY MARKETS

Right there, for the average performing practice, that's 6 potential percentage points of EBITDA that could be used to increase EBITDA from 14% to 20%. It may take a lot of baby steps and a few major steps for a practice to become more efficient in labor and benefits, while continuing to deliver the quality of care that the clients and their pets are accustomed to.

Over recent years, median EBITDA multiples of mergers and acquisitions have been creeping up across almost all industries, not just veterinary.

In 2010 the typical EBITDA multiple across all industries was about 8X. By 2013 it had crept up to 10X, and by 2016 it was at 11X as the median for all merger and acquisition (M&A) activity in the country. As the saying goes, a rising tide lifts all boats.

Median EBITDA multiples of US M&A (including PE buyouts)

2016 has seen an uptick in healthcare and IT activity, two sectors that tend to trade at higher EV/EBITDA multiples due to their perceived high potential for growth, so that contributes to the increase.

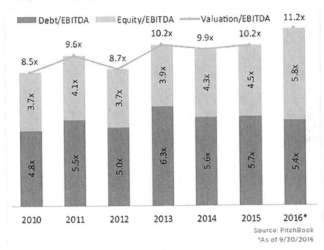

Source: PitchBook
*As of 9/30/2016

In the veterinary space, there have been some deals trading significantly higher than the median level of 11X, with several big deals recently.

The irony is, for a corporate investor, they will pay more for cash flow, EBITDA, the greater that EBITDA is on an absolute level, not a relative level. For example, a large institutional investor with a billion dollars to spend would have to make 1,000 deals at a million dollars each to invest all the money.

In the veterinary business, managing 1000 hospitals would be extremely difficult to scale up effectively and efficiently. It is far easier for the institutional investor to invest that same capital in large chunks and pay up in terms of the EBITDA valuations it chooses to invest in.

By way of reference, some of those big deals you've heard about are mind-numbingly large. Summit Partners sold to National Veterinary Associates (NVA) for $920 million, at 13X EBITDA. BC Partners paid $8.2 billion for PetSmart Inc, at a valuation of about 9X EBITDA.

Incidentally, as you may know, PetSmart had a major role in the growth of Banfield. As PetSmart expanded throughout the U.S., Banfield expanded with a practice and DVMs in every PetSmart. At some point after BC Partners (a private equity group) acquired PetSmart, the investors model changed this growth trajectory. BC Partners as a Private Equity Group (PEG) was not seeking growth, they were seeking cash flow.

Basically they wanted to milk the cow and enjoy the cash flow from PetSmart. Now they would no longer be rolling out new locations, setting off a chain of potentially unintended consequences for Banfield. Now Banfield could no longer grow by expanding their PetSmart footprint. This triggered Banfield to change its business model and reach out to acquire existing practices and hospitals. And now, of course, we've seen what has transpired.

In the interim, there have been plenty of other deals. A private equity firm sold PetVet Care to the Ontario Teachers Pension Plan for $440 million, a valuation of 11X EBITDA. That was in early 2015.

Then, of course, in May of 2016 we saw VCA acquire 80% of Companion Animal Practices of North America (CAPNA) for $344 million.

And finally, among recent big deals, Mars Petcare, parent of Banfield, acquired VCA for $9.1 billion in September of 2017. Mars paid over 3+ times sales to acquire VCA, whose sales were $2.5 billion in 2016. You can understand why VCA was happy to acquire hospitals at 100% (or more) of gross receipts, as they were in discussions with Mars at 3+ times gross receipts.

Wouldn't you like to get an offer for your practice at 3 times your collections? That would be nice.

And in terms of EBITDA, the transaction occurred at an eye-opening multiple of approximately 18X.

So now we've identified what's been going on. It really boils down to this: driven by the need for investors to get a return on their investment, they are seeking reliable high cash flow, and they've found a safe space in the veterinary community.

Take a step back and envision how you would like to see the future of your practice. Is there an associate on your team who can lead the practice when you are no longer there?

If not, can you groom a successor internally or will you have to make a succession plan with a corporate investor? Many hospitals have grown to a size where they may be too large for an associate to be comfortable with the amount of debt necessary to acquire the hospital.

At some point, whether it is 1 year, or 9 years out there will come a time for you to step away from active practice.

What steps can you do today to improve your cash flow?

Who will be the new owner of your hospital or clinic?

Now is the time to make a plan for yourself and your family.

Chapter 4

CORPORATE LOBBYING

"You have family-owned businesses that have been around for 500 years. You cannot name a corporation that survives intact for even a few decades."

--Nassim Nicholas Taleb

Where did corporations come from?

As far as we know, the first corporations were formed in 16th century England as charters from the monarchy which offered the corporate promoter the opportunity to engage in commerce of a specific nature, typically a project with a specific duration, such as building a canal. Once the project was completed, the reason for the corporation ceased to exist, and the charter was terminated.

By law, corporations are designated as "legal persons," thus giving them rights as "persons" even though they are not human beings. Interestingly enough, early on, the Commonwealth of Massachusetts restricted the number of allowed corporations to about a dozen. The legislators of the day were reluctant to issue corporate charters to anyone, out of concern that the actual people behind the corporation could "hide behind the corporate veil" and engage with impunity in activities which they would not be able to do safely as individuals. So in order to avoid "moral hazards," which are situations where there is a lack of incentive to guard against risk because one is protected from its consequences, the average person could not get a corporate charter.

Today, things have gone full circle. People can simply go on the internet and easily and inexpensively file paperwork, select a state of their choosing, and voila! They now have a corporation.

However, all too often these "fill in the box" methods fall far short of assuring compliance with regulatory requirements, especially in cases where one individual is the sole shareholder, the sole employee, and holds each officer role. Oftentimes in this situation corporate minutes are not maintained nor are other legal requirements met. In the event of litigation, the plaintiff suing the corporation will often sue the individual shareholder as well, by "piercing the corporate veil." This basically alleges that the corporation is merely the alter ego of the owner/shareholder, and that the corporation was set up so the shareholder could avoid legal responsibility for actions taken.

In many situations, the veil can be pierced, and individual liability can be found, so beware of setting up a corporation on the internet and/or not meeting regulatory requirements such as meetings and minutes, or any other legal requirements which pertain to your business.

Today we live in a world where corporations have a disproportionate amount of power and influence compared to the early times. If we look way back to the words of Aristotle, "Man is by nature a political animal."

My way of modernizing Aristotle's observation would be to paraphrase it as "A corporation is a political animal."

Now we want to look at corporate activity as it pertains to human medicine. There exists a very large and effective political lobby in Washington, D.C. controlled by corporate America and its financial interest in human medicine. The media everywhere bombard us with streams of commercials and pages of ads regarding drugs, potions, and elixirs of all types, with lists of disclaimers of side effects that may remind us of a Saturday Night Live skit or satire from The Onion. But this is no joke, it's very real.

With many of these ads, the general populace really doesn't know what is being talked about, and the commercial will have a call to action telling us to ask our doctor if the "little red pill" is right for us. It is interesting to note that the U.S. and New Zealand are the only countries that allows prescription medicines to be advertised on TV.

The lobbying efforts and success of corporate America are astounding, and they have an amazing Return on Investment (ROI).

A study by the Center for Public Integrity points out that over the long term blue chip stocks have averaged an 11% compounded annual return.

The Amazing ROI of Lobbying:
Return on Investment

An Ordinary American *Invests in one* BLUE CHIP STOCK	Big Fossil *Lobbies for* OIL SUBSIDIES	Multinationals *Lobby for a corporate* TAX BREAK	Big Pharma *Lobbies to keep* DRUG PRICES HIGH
ROI: 11%	ROI: 5,900%	ROI: 22,000%	ROI: 77,500%

Sources: Center for Public Integrity (data)   United Republic (graphics)

Now look at lobbying returns, for oil/energy companies. The government subsidies they have enjoyed from their lobbying have produced an incredible ROI, in this case a return on their lobbying expenses, of over 5900%. That is $59 for every dollar spent.

If we slither up the lobbying chain a little further, and look at multinational companies generally, and their lobby for tax breaks, we see that every lobbying dollar they spent has an ROI of 22,000%. That is $220 for every dollar spent. Again this is from the Center for Public Integrity.

But the industry that really takes the cake for all of corporate lobbying is Big Pharma. They lobby to keep drug prices high and regulations in their favor. Their ROI is 77,500% --- an astounding return of $775 for each dollar spent on lobbying.

I have no independent way of verifying these figures, but I will say that I think we know there's truth somehow embedded in this research by the Center for Public Integrity.

We don't know what the future effect of lobbying by corporate America might be on the veterinary community. It might be a little too early to draw conclusions, but if it's anything like what we've seen on the human medicine side, I think it's fair to say we might expect to see somewhat more of the same corporate behavior as in other industries.

Looking a bit deeper into pharmaceutical developments affecting human medicine, we can see that the costs are staggering. Typically it takes 10 to 15 years to develop a new drug. There is a very high failure rate. Each new drug costs on average about $2.6 billion. This is from the Tufts Center for the Study of Drug Development (CSDD) study released in late 2014.

Take a look at the cost of pharmaceuticals at your practice and how this impacts the client.

Chapter 5

PROFIT MOTIVE AND CLINICAL RESULTS

"The corporate lobby in Washington is basically designed to stifle all legislative activity on behalf of consumers."

--Ralph Nader

There's an old joke about accountants.

A self-employed businessman has a meeting with his accountant, to talk about "the number."

The businessman asks, "Well, tell me! Tell me! What is it? What's 'the number?'"

The accountant goes over to the window, looks over his shoulder to the left and then to the right, closes the blinds, sits back down, smiles, and asks the businessman: "What do you want it to be?"

When we look at the funded research in the corporate pharma world on the human side, we see a little bit of that behavior. There have been a number of articles, information from whistleblowers, and outright leaks regarding how funded research cherry-picks desired results.

British physician and academic Ben Goldacre has been especially prolific in his writings on this subject, including his book <u>Bad Pharma</u> and numerous articles. He discusses how clinical trial data on new drugs is systematically withheld from doctors and patients, bringing into question many of the practices of the pharmaceutical industry and the integrity of the products it produces.

We're talking about the temptations which can and do arise, in an industry that has large sums riding on the success of a drug after 15 years of development and $2.6 billion spent, on average. It is no surprise that the results of clinical trials might just somehow get skewed when they are reported, if they are reported at all.

Cardiologist Peter Wilmshurst, who blew the whistle on malpractice by a U.S. pharmaceutical company, stated in an interview with the German publication Der Spiegel in an article titled "Positive Results are Better for Your Career," "I can't tell you exactly what the percentage of the trials are flawed. But I think the problem is far bigger than you imagine and getting worse."

Not only does it seem easy to manipulate data, conceal it, or fabricate it, but there is almost a code of silence not to talk about it. It's a travesty, but it is what it is.

Consider also comments from Dr. Marcia Angell, who stated: "It is simply no longer possible to believe much of the clinical research that is published or to rely on the judgment of trusted physicians or authoritative medical guidelines. I take no pleasure in this conclusion which I reached slowly and reluctantly over my two decades as an editor of The New England Journal of Medicine."

These are some shocking observations, all coming from people of impeccable repute in their professions.

No wonder the lay community has so many skeptics regarding big medicine. Many lay people sense there is something not quite right, however they cannot put their finger on it.

As to corporate activity with respect to veterinary medicine, we don't know what will transpire; however when we look at veterinary pharmaceutical development, for example, as compared to human development, it usually takes 3 to 6 years to bring a drug to market, vs. 15 years on the human side. The drug discovery time itself may be cut in third to 1 or 2 years vs. 6 or 7 years on the human side.

Instead of clinical trials as on the human side, we have pivotal studies. Then for the FDA CVM final review and market launch, the approvals might only take 1 or 2 years. So at each stage of the entire process the required duration on the veterinary side is a fraction of that on its human counterpart.

Pharmaceutical Development – Comparison of Animal and Human Medicine

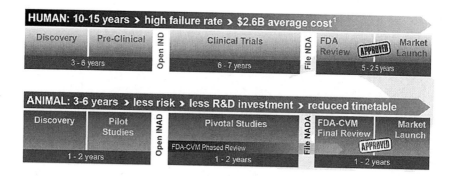

¹ PhRMA 2015 R&D Chartpack, The Biopharmaceutical Research and Development Process

Also, it is interesting to note that on the human side, ultimately drugs are largely paid for by the health insurance industry, or government programs such as Medicare or Medicaid.

In contrast, on the veterinary side, we don't have those sources to pay for our animals' drugs. As pet insurance becomes more commonplace, we'll have to see how this all develops.

dvm360 asked veterinary practitioners what are the veterinary community's top ten most pressing Issues. They are:

TOP TEN MOST PRESSING ISSUES

1. Rising cost and affordability of veterinary care.

2. Competition from non-traditional providers, such as big box, online pharmaceuticals, etc.

3. Client non-compliance, i.e. the reality that clients are not complying with treatment plans.

4. The amount and cost of veterinary school debt, now averaging close to $180,000 for new graduates.

5. Perceived oversupply of practitioners in some areas, and undersupply in others.

6. The perception that Dr. Google and other sources may be purveyors of misinformation.

7. Government regulation, fees and taxes.

8. (Tie)

   a. Corporate practices.

   b. Slippage of veterinarians' strong reputation.

9. Maintaining wellness and preventative care for pets'

10. (Tie)

    a. Poor abilities, attitude and client-handling skills of associates.

    b. Emotional stress, work/life balance, compassion fatigue, and burnout.

So, as seen in concern #8, corporate ownership is on the radar. While it is not the most pressing issue, it may be of great interest for many practice owners who may not be in a position to sell to anyone else.

One of the factors in business which I believe the veterinary community has largely been shielded from is "bad behavior" from the "underbelly" of the corporate world.

Sure, DVMs have been exposed to corporations via their vendor relationships. And there are many fine, decent people who are employed by the corporations we do business with. However, there exists a certain factor within all too many corporate executives and this is not discussed in polite company.

Beware the psychopath on the other side of the table! Several studies are out there which purport the conclusion that approximately 12% of corporate executives are psychopaths. So let's call it 1 out of 8.

In my Wall Street experience, I believe the percentage of psychopaths may be even higher. These fine folks may not have what we may consider to be a conscience. They will tell you anything, fingers crossed behind their backs, thinking it is ok as long as they get what they want.

The veterinary community, for the most part, has had the luxury of not having to deal with this type of animal.

Sure, we've all dealt with corporate reps in our vendor relationships; however, veterinarians typically have not been widely exposed to the executive leadership during a merger or acquisition scenario.

If you are like many of the veterinarians across the country today you a likely receiving multiple letters from various corporate suitors. Many doctors get involved in conversations with the folks making these inquiries, and some wind up representing themselves in a practice transition, for whatever reason.

Most attorneys do not represent themselves in business negotiations or litigation, because they know that their emotions will cloud their thinking and get in the way of their own best interests as it pertains to decision making. They even have an old saying, "An attorney who represents himself has a fool for a client."

This prudent observation should apply to selling a veterinary enterprise as well. Of course, every organization and situation is different, and we have to take each person individually, case by case.

Sometimes you can speak with 20 corporate executives in a row without running into a psychopath. At other times you might find two in a row.

Unfortunately, some are so good at lying we may not find out until it is too late! If you are dealing with a corporate executive who is too smooth or who sets off your "spidey sense" then beware. Get any and all promises in writing with remedies clearly spelled out.

My own theory is that most veterinarians have been somewhat immune to encountering the psychopathic type of potentially dangerous animal. This may be because vets have been surrounded by people who are attracted to the healing and taking care of animals. These people by their nature seem to have innate senses of empathy, awareness of others' needs, and they have a conscience.

A corporate executive I know got very comfortable with sharing some specific detailed information regarding his company's acquisition plans. I like to listen to others, and because I learn more when they are talking I let them go on, as I did in this case.

As he described his views on the veterinary industry, and the opportunities it presented for his company, this fellow couldn't stop talking about how much money his company was making and would make in the future. And then he went down a path that made me uncomfortable as he referred to people as "sheeple."

If you are in the position where the most likely buyer will be a corporate investor, then what steps can you take today to best position yourself accordingly?

Start making a plan and an Exit Plan checklist today.

Start with your values and what you would like to accomplish.

Chapter 6

OWNERSHIP AND THE ASSOCIATE

"I'm a big fan of small business ownership.
I think it's the backbone of American innovation.
But to be successful, you first have to have the
courage to go for it."

-- Bill Rancic

Most practices do not have an associate waiting in the wings seeking practice ownership, and the number of other individual buyers for practices is limited at best.

Some doctors cannot imagine themselves not practicing. Some might envision themselves practicing medicine until they pass on. They are passionate about the things they do.

Many would not know what to do if they retired. Other DVMs would like to ease back from their 6 days per week schedules.

A wise doctor once said about transitioning from active practice, "You'll know when it's time."

A DVM approached me after one of my talks and said, "It's time."

As a sole practitioner with two locations in a beautiful, rural foothill "California Gold Country" community, his sale will not be expected to be a quick and easy because the area is too small to be of interest to a corporate acquirer, and too few DVMs are seeking practice ownership in our smaller communities. Like most vets he did not become a DVM because he was attracted to business matters and HR challenges. He saw fixing animals as his life's work.

This gentleman's two locations would be prime for a DVM to come to town and take over. (So if you know of someone seeking a vet practice in a beautiful setting near hiking, skiing, and lakes, let me know!)

The sole practitioner without an associate has an ongoing challenge. Many DVMs prefer not to have an associate. They may have tried that unsuccessfully in the past.

One strategy that has worked for some is the doctor "sponsoring" their vet tech through veterinary school, sort of like in the olden days when an apprenticeship might run for seven years before obligations were satisfied and journeymanship began. In this case the vet tech returns to the clinic as a DVM.

If I was a young passionate vet tech and someone offered me a "sponsorship" I'd definitely be intrigued.

Frankly, this is a compelling strategy and is probably not utilized nearly to the extent that it should be.

If you have a "super tech" where this could work out, more power to you both! I know one doctor who owned a condo in the university town where the tech attended vet school. As a student she stayed at the condo with the rent deferred until she graduated and came back to the clinic. So now he had an associate who was a known quantity, returning home to work as a DVM. Seems like a pretty sweet story to me!

I think everyone benefits from the "sponsorship" arrangement. Unfortunately, not everyone has the super tech and the timeline where these stars can come into alignment.

Considering that approximately two thirds of households have animals, I contend that two of the greatest challenges facing our communities across the country will continue to be 1) the retirement of sole practitioners; and 2) attracting associates to fill their shoes.

Given those factors, if you are planning to exit your practice, and you are a practice owner, you may really have no realistic alternative but to entertain a corporate buyer. And then you need to meet the criteria the investors seek. So you may have multiple hurdles.

dvm360 conducted a survey which showed the following about how veterinarians feel about corporate ownership on a personal level:

35% strongly oppose

24% somewhat oppose

28% neutral

9% somewhat favor

4% strongly favor

Thus, only 13% of the respondents view corporate ownership favorably.

Obviously the vast majority of veterinarians are not in favor of the tides which seem to be moving towards corporate ownership.

Currently, of the roughly 26,000 veterinary practices in the U.S., it is believed that 10-15% of all animal hospitals are corporate-owned. These are primarily divided among 15 to 20 companies, according to Brakke Consulting. Now that Mars Petcare, parent of Banfield, has completed its acquisition of VCA and its nearly 800 animal hospitals, along with its other chains Mars will own nearly 2000 locations. This represents about two-thirds of all corporate-owned practices.

This begs the question as to the direction in which things might be headed. Ultimately, demographics drive markets. On average, a DVM practice owner is over age 55. A lot of veterinarians don't have an exit strategy. They are passionate about the work they do, and they're in no hurry to retire.

Frankly, for a lot of the doctors I work with, the work they do, and their practice itself, constitutes their very identity, who they really are, at least in their minds. And those are the only minds that count in this equation.

At work, they are the doctor. At home, well....they're not. Most doctors don't see themselves retiring and drinking coffee, sitting around reading the newspaper, golfing or traveling etc. on a full-time basis. They would rather be treating and healing animals than be retired or "put out to pasture."

However, life, being what it is, sometimes has a plan for us, and it may not be one that we would have chosen. Things change, and I impress upon veterinarians that it is in their best interest to have an exit plan, even if they'd like to continue working until they're 80 years old. Things can happen that we cannot anticipate, so it's critically important to have contingency plans.

Practice ownership aspirations have changed dramatically in the last two generations. Currently, according to another survey from dvm360, 70% of all respondents reply NO when asked about practice ownership being one of their aspirations. 38% of men said they would like to own a practice, while only 24% of women said the same.

The survey went a bit deeper, and asked "If no, why not?" 9% of the NOs said they'd already been a practice owner and were planning to retire or phase out of ownership. 14% said they had too much debt already. 22% said "I just want to focus on practicing medicine." But of the vast majority of those who said NO, 43% said "Ownership would just take up too much of my personal time."

So we've clearly seen the life-work balance issue come into the veterinary space in a major way.

For those 30% who do aspire to be a practice owner, when asked "Well, how will you do it?" 39% said they would like to buy into their current practice. Another 17% would like to buy another practice. Roughly a third said they'd like to actually start a new practice. When you add up these figures, it really leaves very little in terms of interest in purchasing an existing practice from a third-party seller.

Now let's examine some of the implications we might derive from this current state of affairs.

Given that so few doctors would like to go out and purchase an existing practice, the path to corporate ownership seems that it will be well-traveled. This appears inevitable, and it is what it is.

We see an ongoing corporate-driven consolidation in the veterinary space, and the vet space is not alone, in a historical context.

Looking back to the early 1900s, in North America there were over 125 different carriage manufacturers, which transitioned from horse drawn carriages to become a very fragmented group of motor carriage manufacturers, and ultimately were consolidated in GM, Ford, and Chrysler and a very few other minor players. So in the auto industry we went from what economists refer to as monopolistic competition to an oligopoly, which is basically a handful of participants in a given market space.

In the veterinary world, we have had widespread monopolistic competition, with a large number of competitors, many of which have relatively few local competitors for the same clientele. At some point, we may have fewer owners for all of the practices. This remains to be seen.

Another factor is that in corporate America the primary way a company can maintain its stock price is through growth. And that has produced an ever-increasing emphasis on mergers and acquisitions, because it is far easier to purchase growth than to create it internally via organic growth.

If we look back at the number of publicly held companies in the U.S. in 1990, there were about 8000 trading on our stock exchanges. Today that number is closer to 4000. About half of the publicly held companies have been acquired by others, or in a few cases gone private or met their demise for one reason or another.

Exhibit 2: Number of Public Companies in the United States

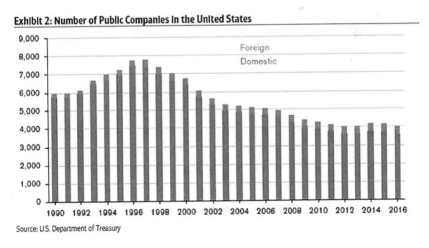

Source: U.S. Department of Treasury

Are there other niche businesses similar to veterinary practices which we might compare in order to draw conclusions?

Perhaps there might be another area in medicine potentially comparable, one where the insurance companies do not control the paycheck as in human medicine? It has been observed that medical doctors largely lost control of their paychecks when they allowed the insurance companies to make that determination on their behalf.

Can you think of any other medical space to which the corporations have been attracted? I would point you to the dental space, where there has been an ongoing consolidation. Possibly up to 30% of the dental market has been rolled up into the corporate world. If you recall from a previous chapter, the Ontario Teachers Pension Plan invested $440 million in the veterinary space. They made a similar investment in the dental space in the U.S.

People reading this might say, wait a minute! Dentists get paid from insurance companies, the same as MDs. This is true; however, when you look into it, our dental insurance benefits have been capped at $1,500 for the last 30+ years. So the impact of insurance on dentistry has been limited.

The first medical practices I brokered were in the "dental industry." Ironically, it is very similar to the veterinary field.

When you attend the exhibitor hall at either a dental conference or a veterinary conference you see the same two large publicly held supply vendors, Henry Schein and Patterson. You see the same lenders who focus on practice finance. And when you visit a dental or veterinary clinic you often see the same dental and imaging equipment.

However, one of the major differences is the attitude held by the associates in regard to practice ownership. For whatever reason, there exists a very strong interest from associate dentists in practice ownership.

Many associates will respond to a practice listing and they will tell me, "Joe, you have to help me. I have to get out of this place, I cannot take it any longer. Please."

Usually it turns out they are working for a corporately owned and managed dental clinic. Many are ordered not to have any small talk with the patient, presumably out of concern that the patient will follow the associate when the associate leaves or is driven out by the corporate culture. Many dental associates burn out quickly from the grueling corporate "factory" approach. Many are disillusioned with "treatment plans" which some have said may more resemble "over-treatment plans." These dental associates seek the opportunity to work for themselves, so they can practice medicine their way, instead of according to some remote corporate committee's rules about how they will more profitably treat the patient. I know this is potentially incendiary language; however, it is what I hear directly from the associates themselves.

In fairness, it can be argued that part of the reason why there is such a chasm in the attitudinal preference towards ownership by dental associates vs. veterinary associates may very well lie in entrepreneurial and perhaps cultural predisposition.

It has been observed that the fastest growing sector of our population in the U.S who are becoming millionaires are first generation Americans. In California, at least, the majority of the dental associates responding to practice opportunities were born in other countries. They come to America to practice dentistry and to do well financially.

In contrast, the vast majority of veterinary students were born in the U.S. and are not attracted to veterinary medicine primarily for economic reasons. Ironically, many veterinarians have done very well economically, however this was not necessarily by design. They simply wanted to treat and heal animals.

Even though this is true for the vast majority of veterinarians, you may have within your staff an associate with an underlying latent proclivity towards practice ownership. Neither you nor they may be aware of their potential entrepreneurial spirit. Maybe at your next staff meeting, should business matters come up, take an informal poll by show of hands and ask the question, "Did any of you have a lemonade stand when you were a kid?"

This simple question just might uncover a potential successor, already on your team.

Chapter 7

VALUATION VS. PRICE DISCOVERY

"A cynic is a man who knows the price of everything and the value of nothing."

-- Oscar Wilde

Every day veterinary practice owners get a day closer to retiring. We are all approaching our "best if used before date," some of us sooner than others.

At some point, it's likely you'll eventually be transitioning from active practice. And if you're like most doctors, you just don't have the time to dig in and research the process of selling your practice and transitioning out.

To avoid potentially very costly mistakes, you'd like to getter a better, firm understanding of the transition process. You'd like to learn important information about just what is involved, and that may be part of the reason why you're reading this book.

One of the key areas is the concept of valuation, and which factors and assumptions ultimately drive valuation to a specific number in the sale of a practice.

If you remember earlier from Chapter 2, we discussed cash flow. Since cash flow is going to be the main driver of your valuation, understanding the elements of cash flow is really going to be the key for you to better position the value of your practice in anticipation of your eventual exit.

You may decide to hire someone to prepare a practice valuation. For that you will need to provide some documents, likely including a minimum of three years business tax return schedules, a listing of the staff compensation, detailed payroll for the most recent year, and profit and loss statements for the last three years (they include more information than tax return schedules).

TAX SCHEDULE

Form **1120S**

U.S. Income Tax Return for an S Corporation

▶ Do not file this form unless the corporation has filed or is attaching Form 2553 to elect to be an S corporation.
▶ Information about Form 1120S and its separate instructions is at www.irs.gov/form1120s.

OMB No. 1545-0123

2016

For calendar year 2016 or tax year beginning _____ , 2016, ending _____ , 20 ____

A S election effective date	Name: Your Animal Hospital	D Employer identification number
B Business activity code number (see instructions)	Number, street, and room or suite no. If a P.O. box, see instructions. 123 Main St.	E Date incorporated
C Check if Sch. M-3 attached	City or town, state or province, country, and ZIP or foreign postal code: Anytown, USA	F Total assets (see instructions)

G Is the corporation electing to be an S corporation beginning with this tax year? ☐ Yes ☐ No If "Yes," attach Form 2553 if not already filed
H Check if: (1) ☐ Final return (2) ☐ Name change (3) ☐ Address change (4) ☐ Amended return (5) ☐ S election termination or revocation
I Enter the number of shareholders who were shareholders during any part of the tax year ▶
Caution: Include only trade or business income and expenses on lines 1a through 21. See the instructions for more information.

Income		
1a Gross receipts or sales	1a 1,200,000	
b Returns and allowances	1b	
c Balance. Subtract line 1b from line 1a	1c	1,200,000
2 Cost of goods sold (attach Form 1125-A)	2	305,000
3 Gross profit. Subtract line 2 from line 1c	3	
4 Net gain (loss) from Form 4797, line 17 (attach Form 4797)	4	
5 Other income (loss) (see instructions—attach statement)	5	
6 Total income (loss). Add lines 3 through 5 ▶	6	895,000

Deductions (see instructions for limitations)		
7 Compensation of officers (see instructions—attach Form 1125-E)	7	120,000
8 Salaries and wages (less employment credits)	8	288,000
9 Repairs and maintenance	9	
10 Bad debts	10	
11 Rents	11	72,000
12 Taxes and licenses	12	
13 Interest	13	8,000
14 Depreciation not claimed on Form 1125-A or elsewhere on return (attach Form 4562)	14	30,000
15 Depletion (Do not deduct oil and gas depletion.)	15	
16 Advertising	16	24,000
17 Pension, profit-sharing, etc., plans	17	25,000
18 Employee benefit programs	18	
19 Other deductions (attach statement)	19	34,000
20 Total deductions. Add lines 7 through 19 ▶	20	
21 Ordinary business income (loss). Subtract line 20 from line 6	21	294,000

The person performing the valuation will need your depreciation schedule, and a list of assets. Usually you can pull the list of assets right off the depreciation schedule. It shows what was purchased, when, at what price, and the year actually put into service.

And remember, it's all about cash flow. We talked about EBITDA earlier, and that will be the driving force. That's what the corporate buyer, or likely the lender in the case of an individual buyer, will be evaluating.

The person performing the valuation will start with your tax return and then add back the Interest, Taxes, Depreciation, and Amortization, the I-T-D-A of EBITDA.

But then they will go further. To make the numbers look like they might for a new owner's scenario, they need to back out any current owner-related discretionary expenses. A buyer will add back personal benefits, personal discretionary travel, and perhaps luxury auto expenses. The rationale for this is that the new owner would not necessarily have to incur these expenses. The same might apply for continuing education expenses and meals. For an individual buyer they might also add back the owner's salary to see the total cash flow to pay themselves, service the debt and paydown some of the principal each year.

When the I-T-D-A and discretionary items have been added back, we now have arrived at adjusted cash flow, technically, "adjusted EBITDA."

Adjustments to Taxable Income

Net Receipts per Tax Return	$ 2,278,298
Expenses per Tax Return	2,099,248
Profit per Tax Return	179,050
Add Back:	
Owner's Salaries	114,300
Legal fees (normalized)	
Consulting Fees	24,000
Meals and Entertainment	1,167
Interest	5,053
Rents (normalized)	
Charitable Donations	
Auto and Parking Expense	1,000
Dues & Subscriptions	3,730
Gifts	
Advertising	15,000
Depreciation	8,886
Amortization	
Continuing Education/Professional Development	3,701
Pension & Profit Sharing	9,904
Travel & Transportation	4,575
Adjusted Net Income	$ 370,366

In addition, if you own the building, you may be holding the real estate in a separate legal entity. Perhaps a professional corporation or LLC is holding the practice, and another might be holding the real estate.

The rent which the practice is paying may or may not represent fair market value rent for your community. For tax planning purposes it's possible you're paying higher or lower rent than what fair market value might be. If either of those is true, the rent needs to be hypothetically "normalized" in the calculations used to value the practice. In other words, the rent needs to be adjusted to the approximate fair market value in your area, because that is presumably the situation the buyer would be in. It's not always an easy question to answer, depending on your community and the dynamics of your practice.

In addition, the person performing the valuation will need to make adjustments for any other unusual expenses, such as one-time expenses. Perhaps last year there was a large one time only legal bill, and that bill will not be anticipated to occur next year or in the foreseeable future. So, it gets added back in for the calculation. This type of "one off" item is what you've heard being called a "non-recurring" item.

So valuation is an important concept, and one needs to apply both art and science to what are often very complicated factual situations.

But, at the end of the day, valuation is one thing, and the price a practice will actually sell for is another. In the marketplace, price is really whatever a willing buyer will pay and what a willing seller will accept. That is known as "price discovery."

Ultimately though, it may not really matter what the valuation report says.

Recently a doctor asked me, "what is the multiple for a practice nowadays?" In this case they preferred to sell the practice to an associate rather than being forced to go down the corporate path. Then the doctor asked me, "What's the average or typical discount for an owner selling to an associate?"

I replied, "When you think about it, price is price. It doesn't matter if the buyer is an associate, it doesn't matter if the buyer is a corporate entity or an investor. The price is whatever you're willing to sell for and whatever they're willing to pay." Price discovery takes two parties to agree on a single price.

The single best way to determine price is through an auction. You gather the interested buyers and let them bid. Warren Buffett hates auctions and chooses not to participate in them because he knows he will get emotionally involved with his bidding.

As a side note, many men in Amish communities are contractors/carpenters. When it is time for them to retire and sell their tools/business they have an auction. The eldest son of the seller is expected to be the best bidder. So that is an interesting answer and approach to the question as to how you determine value. Let the marketplace "discover the price." That way the patriarch of the family gets a fair price and the adult child does not get a handout.

Many doctors feel strongly about selling to an associate, and they will offer a meaningful discount from the price that a corporate investor might pay.

Probably the most common reason for this is that the associate may have been on board for many years and the doctor wants to show their gratitude because the associate helped build the practice and its goodwill. Also, a strong preference for not having any corporate buyer in the picture may factor into this decision. Hence the discount, and smooth continuity for the practice.

However, sometimes, the premium being dangled by the corporate investor is greater than anticipated. This can create some real challenges when there had been a verbal understanding between the doctor and the associate that the associate would be buying the practice at some point.

If and when the doctor receives a corporate offer that they think they cannot refuse, the associate is effectively shut out. This scenario has led to many business problems, legal disputes, and broken friendships.

Another factor to keep in mind about valuation is that individual buyers are often constrained by financial resources, and they can only afford the purchase if a bank extends a sufficient loan. Corporate investors and private equity funds do not have this constraint.

Some creative financing may potentially solve this issue.

If the bank will lend X, but the corporate entity is willing to pay X+20%, one way around the corporate sale could be that the individual buyer borrows X and the seller carries back a loan for the additional 20%.

When economic times are lean the bank lenders may not be there, and the seller will typically finance the transaction.

However, it is not usually in the seller's best interest to carry the loan when a bank will do so. There have been situations in which the seller makes the loan and then something happens to the buyer. It is no fun for a doctor who sold their practice to an associate and "retired", and then something happens, and the doctor has to return to active practice. So when the lenders are willing, there is really no reason for a seller to carry the loan.

If you have ever made a comment to an associate who is anticipated to be your potential successor, and if you suggested that you would or might be able to carry the loan, then this might be a good time to revisit and clarify this subject.

Feel free to contact me, and I can introduce your associate to an appropriate lender specializing in the veterinary space.

Chapter 8.

LENDERS

"Banks need to continue to lend to creditworthy borrowers to earn a profit and remain strong."

-- Ben Bernanke

Hank was a veterinarian from Nebraska and he needed a loan. He drove his new RV to New York City, walked into a bank and told the loan officer he was not a customer but needed to go to Paris for two weeks and needed a $10,000 loan.

The loan officer said they would need some security for the loan, so Hank handed over the keys. The RV was parked on the street in front of the bank. The title checked out ok, so the RV was now collateral for a $10,000 loan at 12%.

Later the bank's president and officers all enjoyed a good laugh at Hank the veterinarian from Nebraska for using a $300,000 RV as collateral for a $10,000 loan. A bank employee then drove the RV into the bank's private garage and parked it.

Two weeks later, Hank returned, and repaid the $10,000 plus interest of $46.15.

The loan officer said, "We are very happy to have had your business, and this transaction worked out very nicely, but we are a little puzzled."

He continued, "While you were away, we checked you out on Dun & Bradstreet and found that you are a distinguished alumnus from the University of Nebraska, a sophisticated investor and multi-millionaire with real estate and significant investments throughout the Midwest, including a number of veterinary hospitals and a large ranch with oil wells."

"What puzzles us is, why would you bother to borrow $10,000?"

And Hank, the good 'ole vet from Nebraska replied,

"Where else in New York City can I park my RV for two weeks for only $46.15 and expect it to be there when I return?"

Lenders love veterinarians.

There exists a handful of banks focused on lending to professional medical practitioners, providing liquidity and capital to veterinarians. In fact, the veterinarian community has been an excellent credit risk for these lenders. These banks have experienced about a quarter of 1% of default risk on the loans made by them to vets. That is .25 %, which means 99.75% of the loans made to DVMs perform.

Can you think of an industry with a higher success rate? I was told by a vet that his banker told him years ago that the only profession with a lower failure rate is funeral directors. It is interesting to note that the banks' experience in lending to MD's has resulted in significantly higher default rates than those for loans to veterinarians. In short, the banks *really* like the stability and growth of veterinary practice cash flow.

I should also mention the Small Business Administration (SBA). If a DVM goes to a local bank seeking capital to purchase a practice and/or the real estate, the lender will often push for an SBA loan. I think this is unfortunate, unnecessary, and even ironic in the sense that if the banking community has had such great experience with veterinarians, why is an SBA loan even being proposed?

If a vet takes out an SBA loan they have to pay up to 3.75% in SBA guaranty fees upfront. That's above and beyond the bank's loan origination fees, and above and beyond the interest they'll be paying every year. If vets are such a good risk, why are they being coerced into paying these extra "guaranty fees?"

The answer is that the veterinary community is subsidizing the risks of other SBA borrowers. And the greatest amount of money being lent through the SBA goes to the fast food industry and independent restaurateurs who may not survive beyond their first year.

So banks love to write SBA loans. They get an origination fee, and then Uncle Sam takes the risk, which really is the taxpayers' risk.

There are some buyers whose credit may not be stellar, and they may not have much choice but an SBA loan, and that's simply the way it is. Others may be acquiring land or a building. By going the SBA route they may be able to do the deal for no money out of pocket. The lender effectively capitalizes the 3%+ guaranty fee and adds it to the loan package. So a borrower with big plans and not much cash in the bank might be a viable candidate for an SBA loan.

I'm not suggesting that the SBA is inherently bad or undesirable. I am suggesting that for the veterinary community, with its low history of defaults, it is a shame that they have to pick up the tab for other industries with significantly higher failure rates. That is all.

When we're talking about buyers we should also talk about the changing demographics in our country. Over 10,000 baby boomers reach retirement age every day. Baby boomers, including everyone 45 years old or older, control approximately 90% of the wealth in the U.S. At some point that 90% will be passing down to the next generations. What interest will the inheritors of that money have in owning veterinary practices? Obviously that remains to be seen.

Another dynamic in our demographics that we haven't really seen until this century is the explosion in student debt, the outstanding amount of which now stands at over a trillion dollars. A young doctor with a family, carrying a major student debt load, and a mortgage and car loan, may very well have neither the appetite nor any foreseeable wherewithal to take on even more debt to purchase or invest in a practice. And that's sad, but certainly understandable.

By the same token though, perhaps the best way to get out of debt *might* actually be by owning a practice. Take on more debt, buy a practice that cash flows very well, then use that cash flow to pay down the acquisition debt, the student loan debt, and the mortgage debt.

It seems counter-intuitive that the fastest way out of debt could be to take on more debt. Ironically, this approach is likely the quickest way for a younger DVM to become debt free. The cash flow from the practice is the key to this plan, and this approach is certainly something to think about very seriously.

If you carry significant levels of student debt which you would love to extinguish, feel free to reach out to me and we can discuss how this might work.

Chapter 9

ASSOCIATE OR INDIVIDUAL PURCHASE

"When the student is ready the teacher will appear."

-- Anonymous

It seems that most practice owners would prefer to sell their hospital or clinic to an individual buyer, yet there are many individual practitioners who would like to slow down or exit active practice entirely for whatever reason. Unfortunately, they may not have an associate or a likely successor.

They may have never had an associate, or if they did, it might have been years ago, and at that time they may have felt frustrated by their perception that perhaps the associate wasn't as talented or efficient as themselves. So in many cases it was easier for the practice owner to "do everything themselves."

For whatever reason, the doctor may have felt that it would be preferable to go it alone without an associate, and now it's been 25 or 30 years since they've had one. This presents a real challenge. Now the doctor must go outside to find an individual buyer seeking a practice, and unfortunately one of the main challenges with individual buyers is that we simply don't have enough of them.

In a previous chapter we saw a DVM in his sixties facing the problem of a shortage of associates that would like to purchase a practice. Therein lies the challenge.

In many locales there seems to be a greater number of DVM practice owners exiting the profession than the supply of new doctors and/or associates considering practice ownership.

Today most of those associates who would like to own a practice want that practice to be near a major metropolitan area.

The younger doctors want good schools, cultural amenities, nightlife, etc. Bottom line: If you're a sole practitioner in a tertiary market, it may be very challenging to find a young doctor to step into your shoes.

In past generations doctors generally had a stronger interest in the outdoor lifestyle, and activities such as fishing or hiking in remote mountains. Those doctors are still out there, of course, but their absolute numbers seeking this lifestyle and practice ownership are fewer.

Who will be the buyer of a practice in a small community or rural area? We see a lot of practices in these areas basically shuttering their doors and windows because the doctors just can't find a buyer for their practice, at least on any kind of timely basis.

I like to believe that there is a buyer for every seller, but in reality the process is far longer for the more rural locations, and the probability of a sale is far less certain.

I would also really like to believe that there is someone from that community or nearby, who went away to college and veterinary school and would like to return to practice in that community, and be near the family they grew up with. So there is hope, but it's just not the same as finding a buyer for a practice in a metropolitan area.

When we have an associate working within the practice who would like to take over the reins, that is an entirely different scenario. In this case, the associate already knows the clients, the patients, the staff, and the systems. One would think this associate is an ideal buyer, and one would probably be right!

Bear in mind, though, that if the practice has multiple DVMs, the likelihood of corporate investor interest increases proportionately with the number of DVMs in the practice.

When that happens, the price the seller may be offered from a corporate investor is probably going to be higher than the amount that traditional lenders would consider extending to the associate as a practice acquisition loan. This is not an opinion of value from the lender, it is more of a loan collateral position the banks prefer to take.

A practice owner told me that he'd rather sell his hospital to his associate.

He said, "She's been with me for 18 years and I'd really like her to take over."

And he then asked me, "What is the average price discount between selling to an associate vs selling to a corporate buyer?"

I explained that price is really whatever a willing buyer and willing seller agree to.

If a corporate investor were to offer you $ X and the associate were to offer you something less than $ X, the decision really comes down to what discount, if any, you would be willing to take.

So, this really is a personal decision, and there is no empirical record or database that has been compiled which can answer the question. Even if there were such a database, or study, any conclusions drawn would likely be of limited value. There are just so many variables unique to the each of the alternatives.

In this case of the 18-year associate, the owner did not feel comfortable in negotiating with her and working through the whole process. So, he engaged me to negotiate an offer with her, and if she elects not to acquire the hospital then we will have to go to the marketplace to find an outside buyer.

The differential between what a corporate buyer might pay vs. what the bank might lend to an associate might be a gap of 15-20% or more on a million-dollar sale.

So, in this hypothetical million-dollar sale, if the lender might lend up to $850,000, and if the seller will carry back a loan for $150,000, the seller and the associate buyer can make the deal happen. The seller has the additional benefit of earning interest on that $150,000 plus perhaps retaining a security interest in the property until the loans are paid off.

A modest amount of seller financing can work in many cases. The seller needs to consider balancing any additional risk for a sale to the associate vs. the perceived impact to the practice and the community for a sale to a corporate investor. If you do not have an "heir apparent" and would like one then it is never too late to try to locate one.

I'm working on a unique approach to solve this challenge and will have an alternative sometime in 2018. Reach out and let me know if this might be of interest to you.

Chapter 10

WHAT ARE CORPORATE BUYERS SEEKING?

"Wide diversification is only required when investors do not understand what they are doing."

-- Warren Buffett

Corporate buyers are generally seeking to acquire veterinary practices with multiple DVMs, with top line gross receipts of $1.3 million or more, because these practices will have sufficient cash flow to provide a reasonable return on their investment.

The reason they seek multiple DVMs is for certainty of client and patient coverage. Imagine if an investor purchased a practice with only one doctor, and something were to happen to that one doctor, now the new non-DVM owner has no revenue production in that practice.

And heaven forbid, if the doctor is unable to return to work, then the corporate owner has the additional risk of recruiting a replacement doctor. So the need for multiple

DVMs is really about risk reduction in addition to enhancing cash flow.

You can understand why corporate buyers are very reluctant to take on those risks, versus mitigating the risk by investing in practices with multiple DVMs.

Recently while speaking to a large group of practice owners at a veterinary conference, I asked for a show of hands from those that received a letter from a corporate investor regarding the potential sale of their hospital or clinic. Nearly everyone raised their hand. Then I asked how many had received two letters, three letters, or four or more.

It was clear that a considerable percentage of the veterinarians in that room had received four or more letters.

There is a correlation between the number of letters you will receive and how many DVMs are listed on your website. The more DVMs, the greater the gross income, the greater the expected net income, and the greater the cash flow to the investor.

The corporate buyer must acquire; acquisition is the mission. This type of buyer seeks the larger practice, and the larger the better.

One doctor came up to me after the presentation and said, "You really blew my mind. We have 14 DVMs and 3 locations. I have never seen a single letter."

"Seen" is the operative word in that sentence. I think it's safe to say some of his partners have "seen" the letters! Maybe they "forgot" to tell him?

At the time of this writing there were about 30 corporate investor/buyers operating in the U.S. Corporate consolidators come in various shapes, sizes, and with all types of backgrounds.

When you think about it, the value of the used equipment at a hospital or clinic is typically modest at best.

So the consolidators are basically buying goodwill, an intangible asset which we cannot touch or see, but has real value, and through multiple DVMs the goodwill factor is leveraged.

Embedded in the invisible asset of goodwill is the expectation that the clients will continue to bring the patients to the hospital or clinic, thereby capturing cash flow for the investor.

As noted, consolidators come in many forms. Some are the traditional large chains we all know of, and we all likely know people who have sold their practices to one of these companies. Many doctors are fine and well with their decision to merge into one of the large traditional chains. Others undoubtedly have not been happy with the process or the outcome.

A wise business person once pointed out, "You notice that when someone sells their business to Warren Buffett they are still working there years later at 85?"

Often someone sells their business with an agreement to continue working for a specified time period. Too often this period of time can sound like a prison sentence when they say something like "I get out of here in two years."

Another type of corporate acquirer you may encounter falls under the category of a "private equity group" or PEG. Basically, a PEG is a professionally managed pool of money. The managers seek investment opportunities to grow the pool of capital while taking risks commensurate with their group's vision and risk tolerance. Typically the capital contributions come from institutions, banks, insurance companies, pension plan savings, and high net worth individuals.

Some of the PEGs have a short duration, maybe five years in some cases, and at that time investors may be cashed out.

Since PEGs typically do have a duration with a fixed lifespan, they must be acquiring and managing in order to be doing their job. Some people liken PEGs to "purchasing agents" for their associated pools of capital.

PEGs typically seek to assemble a portfolio of practices and flip the portfolio to a larger buyer when it is time to wind down. Often the real pros know who they are going to sell to down the road even before they buy businesses for their portfolio.

In the veterinary space, some of the consolidators have been around for many years, while others are brand new and seeing their first acquisition.

One of the challenges right now in the veterinary community is simply finding new associates. A few generations ago, people seemed more in the mode of living to work, vs. today when it could be said that the life-work balance has tipped to where more and more people seek to work to live.

Many of the younger DVMs may want to work only two or three days a week. Many are not seeking to work six days a week, as so many senior doctors did when they started their careers, and indeed in many cases continue to do so throughout their careers, right up to the day they transition out.

Today, almost 80% of today's graduating DVMs are women. Many new female practitioners do not want to make a practice ownership decision until they have established a family, if at all.

Granted, many doctors of both sexes are not attracted to the idea of owning a practice. However, studies show that women are generally less interested in the business and entrepreneurial aspects of owning a veterinary practice when compared to men.

Where are all the graduates going? There are quite a few hospitals aggressively seeking to recruit associates. I recently met with one doctor who has four locations, and wants to acquire another; however, he just doesn't have the labor force to staff another acquisition, and it's not for lack of trying.

This doctor has been advertising aggressively across the country in hopes of finding an associate for the position. He told me he had even asked one potential interviewing associate, "What would you like to get paid? Name your price." He was ready to pay a substantial premium just to get another doctor into his practice.

It cannot be overemphasized that finding associates is a very significant challenge for existing doctors, and it's going to be a challenge for the corporate investors as well.

As stated earlier, corporate investors focus on and seek opportunities where there are multiple DVMs, to protect themselves against the risk of loss of a DVM's services, by disability, death, or whatever reason. In addition, many of the corporate consolidators will seek to pay a selling doctor a staggered payout, say 70% or so of the acquisition price immediately, with the balance of 30% payable down the road, typically in 3-5 years.

The deferred payment incentivizes the seller to remain for an orderly period and to help make the transfer of goodwill more effective. Hopefully this also gives the seller a chance to wind down their busy schedule a bit. That seems to be a common theme. Many doctors who own practices would like to continue working, but perhaps for only two or three days a week, vs. the five or six days they're working now.

One of the other challenges in finding associates pertains to younger doctors just graduating, who for a while may not have the skill set or experience to handle some of the things going on in a typical day at the veterinary clinic. They may have graduated having done only one surgery, and that might have been a spay or neuter.

One doctor told me that she was surprised that the younger docs weren't very sure which lab tests to order even in fairly routine cases. At a clinic where she was a relief DVM, the younger associates were being compensated by a percentage of production, and she noted that they typically ordered the most expensive test when they had several choices, even though that may not have been the most cost-effective choice for the client. They just defaulted to the most expensive test, perhaps presuming it would be the best, but at the same time, knowing it would pay them the most.

Issues like these concern many long-time practitioners and others as they contemplate the effect of the corporate investors entering and disrupting the traditional veterinary practice model.

A veterinarian consulted me about the possible sale of his hospital found himself in a bit of a quandary.

As usually the case, the staff did not know a sale was being considered.

Soon the vet received a sizeable offer from one of the large veterinary corporate chains. The sum was a healthy six figures greater than the next highest proposal.

A couple of his vet techs had worked at one of the local hospitals owned by this suitor and over the months they had been telling other staff stories about "how awful" it had been working there.

The owner was losing sleep and concerned about the consequences of selling to this highest bidder, including the possibility of a staff mutiny. So, he decided to sell to the second highest bidder, a smaller corporate investor type.

So the vet left a considerable amount of money on the table, but the new owner, the smaller corporate type investor, visits once or twice a year and does not micromanage.

The seller remains happy with his decision, and sleeps just fine.

Other doctors have met with corporate representatives seeking to acquire their practice and for whatever reason they did not get a "warm and fuzzy" vibe from the corporation.

Recently I met with a husband and wife who own a practice. They have done very well, and the hospital has grown to quite a substantial size.

This couple had received the letters and calls from corporate acquirers and had agreed to meet with two of them. However, they found that they were really not comfortable with the people with whom they were meeting.

They even received a large offer, $5 million, but things just simply "did not feel right," so they did not want to proceed. So they asked me if I could find an individual buyer.

I explained that it would not be easy, and asked them "May I ask you both a question?" They agreed.

So I then inquired, "Would you, knowing what you know now, and through some combination of hard work, savings and inheritance have $5 million to plunk down on a barrel head ---- would you exchange that for working six days a week and managing a whole bunch of staff ---- would you make that trade.?"

They both shook their heads and emphatically said "No."

Therein lies the challenge. It is true, some DVM somewhere would say "Yes." But it won't be fast or easy to locate that person.

Let me know if you, or someone you know, might be interested in taking on ownership of a large practice in a fast-growing Western city.

If you do not have an associate to step into your shoes, and the corporate buyer is the likely buyer, what steps can you take today to better position yourself for a corporate investor's bid?

This is your opportunity to transition on your terms.

Think about what is most important to you and write it down, review it from time to time and adjust it as your thoughts coalesce.

Chapter 11

PLANNING YOUR EXIT

If you don't know where you are going any road will take you there.

-- Anonymous

How do you get what you want? And if you can't get what you want, then how do you get what you need?

When you make a plan, you have to start with the desired outcome and work backward to the present time. Reverse engineering the baby steps this can be easier to say then to actually do. These ideas take time and effort to brainstorm.

When making your exit plan, if you can envision where you would like to be after active practice, then you know where you want to go. And with that in mind, you now have a basis on which you can begin to negotiate.

Over time things may change, as life has a way of throwing us curve balls. We might have to move to Plan B, or C, or D.

So, make a plan and have backup or contingency plans.

If you're anywhere from one to nine years from transitioning out of active practice, then now is the time to make a plan.

One doctor I was representing said they wished they had started this process five years ago, because there would have been so many things they could have done over that period of time, and now they simply did not have the same amount of time to plan properly.

What steps can you take today to best position yourself for a smooth transition down the road?

That's a question I often get asked, and it's the right question to ask, because if you don't have a plan to get to the finish line, well, there's that old saying, "If you don't have a plan, then life has one for you and it may not be the one of your choosing."

If you know that you would like to transition out in five years or less, there are still plenty of things you can do. Of course, the more time to make changes within your clinic or hospital, the better, but even the best laid plans can be thrown a curveball when something changes in our family life or personal life, and our priorities may unexpectedly shift.

Hopefully, you aren't on the receiving end of life's unexpected turns and you're able to execute your Plan A. However, it is always prudent to have at least one or two contingency plans.

Given that corporate acquirers target practices with multiple DVMs, it is the cash flow that ultimately most influences what a buyer will pay.

Since the "average practice" has cash flow, or EBITDA, of 14% of revenue, a practice with cash flow significantly higher than 14% has a strong likelihood of commanding a premium price compared to an "average practice."

Ideally the corporate buyers want to see very strong cash flow (EBITDA). If a hospital or clinic had EBITDA of 25% that would put the practice within the top 20% of all veterinary practices in the country.

So basically, the gist of the corporate buyer's agenda is twofold: The bigger the better, and the more doctors the better. Because of these factors the cash flow will be very closely examined and will be expected to be very significantly higher than average.

That said, if you're not firing on all cylinders cash flow-wise, there are steps you can take to repair and enhance the value of your practice.

A wise doctor once said, "I don't know one single way to get 100 new patients, but I know 100 ways to get 100 new patients in a month."

I think that's well said, because there is no magic bullet, no easy way that's going to move your EBITDA from 14% to 25%. There are benchmarks the AVMA puts out with their economic reports, and you can see how your practice compares with others.

If your practice is underperforming on a certain bench-mark, say for example cost of goods sold, then you can drill down and compare your data with specific industry-wide benchmarks, and thereby focus on areas where you may need to be more efficient.

If you can gain one percentage point of efficiency in one area, and another point in another area, etc., those points do start to add up. Before you know it, instead of 14% EBITDA you might find yourself at 18%, and the pricing of your prac-tice has now measurably increased.

% of Practice Revenue 2016 AVMA Report on Veterinary Markets		
	Top 20%	All Practices
Direct Costs	20%	22%
Labor & Benefits	40%	46%
Other Expenses	15%	18%
EBITDA	25%	14%

As another example, if your direct costs are at 22%, you're average for that metric. However, a top 20% practice has 20% of revenues going to direct costs. So there might be room for improvement on that score.

Similarly, with regard to labor and benefits, the top 20% spends 40% of revenues, while average is 46%. So working with that six-percentage point differential, if you can get your costs for labor and benefits down to 40%, you can boost your EBITA from 14% to 20% and you're getting closer to the ideal of 25% or greater, and then you're really enhancing the value of your practice.

Practices across the country average 18% of their revenues on "other expenses." The top performers average 15%. There's another opportunity.

As you can see, there are a number of items which can be improved, some easily and others involving more of a challenge, but I'm sure you get the idea.

As a call to action, take a look at your practice, and compare your financial results to the AVMA benchmarks. Then you will see areas where you might be able to improve.

As a side note, most veterinary practice owners typically own the real estate, while corporate investors are not typically attracted to real estate ownership, as they prefer to lease. The reason is that the corporate investor's expected return on capital for a real estate acquisition is considerably less when compared to their expected return for a practice acquisition, thus they allocate their investment funds accordingly.

Should the doctor hold on to the real estate? After all, it can represent a stream of income in terms of lease payments from the new buyer.

On the other hand, the doctor may have some concerns about what happens down the road when the lease expires, and what happens if the buyer chooses not to renew? Maybe the buyer later acquires another practice in a better location on the other side of town? Perhaps they consolidate the facilities in the new location?

Thus, should the practice move out at a later date, for any reason, there is a risk that the property owner may have to repurpose the real estate.

Potential pitfalls like these can be contemplated in the negotiations prior to the sale of the practice, and these are the type of details which I watch for to better position doctors selling their practices, and to best protect their interests, both now and in the future.

While I am a broker in terms of finding and matching buyers and sellers, I am also an advisor to the professional practitioner.

Practice brokerage is really a specialization within the umbrella of general business brokerage, which in turn is regulated by the real estate licensing bureaus in most of the states throughout the country. So I am typically required to be licensed as a real estate broker in a number of states, and also as a business broker in certain jurisdictions accordingly. This is important because real estate is a significant part of my practice brokerage business.

What steps can you take today to best position yourself for a smooth transition down the road?

If you need help getting started on your process, or get buried in the details, feel free to reach out to me.

APPENDIX

"If you fail to plan, you are planning to fail!"

-- Benjamin Franklin

This is a story of unintended consequences.

One evening in mid-December I received a call from a doctor friend who asked me if I would reach out to someone, Kathy, whose surgeon husband and sole practitioner had suddenly passed away unexpectedly. My friend said that Kathy was trying to sell the practice by herself and was in a very tough situation.

In the case of a surgical specialty practice it has been estimated that should the doctor become incapacitated, the practice can lose 10% of its value for every week the practice is closed. If the doctor is not working, the referral sources simply stop referring and the "goodwill" that the practice may have taken years to build can quickly evaporate.

So, with the clock ticking, Kathy was immediately proactive and arranged with several surgeons to provide some continuity to her deceased husband's schedule. She also engaged a well-known attorney with specialization in handling legal aspects of sales of professional practices.

Well, soon one of the surgeons who was filling in expressed an interest in buying the practice. Neither Kathy nor her attorney had any reason to believe that the buyer was not bona fide and did not have sincere intentions.

At least that's how things had appeared at first. But by the time I first spoke with Kathy she explained that she is a surgical nurse with decades of experience, and is normally an emotionally level-headed person, and "does not cry like this."

Well, she explained that as it turned out the purported buyer had started a pattern of coming in and telling Kathy that the deal was off, then the next day the deal was back on, but as this pattern repeated the price kept going lower.

Kathy was extremely distraught; a newly widowed victim being emotionally and financially manipulated by a cruel phony buyer for financial gain.

Amazingly, the "buyer's" wife even told a banker that they were going to "drag their heels and planned to get this practice for nothing."

Now over the prior couple of years Kathy and her husband had built both a beautiful state of the art surgical facility and a custom home. These two properties were to be their last home and office.

While Kathy as a surgical nurse had a reasonably comfortable living, she simply did not, on her own after he husband's death, have the savings and cash flow to pay for all the legal fees, the mortgage on the new home, and the commercial loan payments on the new surgical suite. Her husband had left only a modest life insurance policy, and it would not last long in Kathy's quickly deteriorating financial circumstances.

Moreover, Kathy's husband had not left a will, or any trusts. Now she was going to have to engage an attorney to handle matters of probate. And her husband had an adult son from a previous marriage, who would likely be a beneficiary heir in the probate process.

At this point, with expenses exceeding income, and liabilities possibly exceeding assets, Kathy consulted with a bankruptcy attorney, bringing on even more expense. Kathy's accountant was also brought in, and they determined that if the practice were to be sold by year end she would save over $100,000 in taxes.

Now when selling a practice, the seller provides the buyer with documents showing assets free and clear of encumbrances and transferring ownership to the buyer in exchange for cash at the closing of escrow.

In Kathy's case though, it would be very challenging to sell a practice she did not even have title to, and especially difficult with only two weeks left in the year.

And to make matters even worse, Kathy got a call from the bank which had made the commercial loan. The banker stated that the loan was only for an owner operator, and not an investor. Since Kathy was not a doctor, the banker said she was thus an investor, and in violation of the loan covenants.

The "buyer's" attorney now seemed to be in the "Attorney Protection Program" and was not returning any calls.

It was clear: Kathy needed a new buyer, and NOW! On December 23, Kathy stopped paying her attorney and engaged me to procure a buyer for her husband's practice. Since I work on a success basis, with a commission contingent on an actual sale, Kathy did not have to find any funding in order to engage my efforts.

So..... I had roughly a week to put together and close a sale of a medical practice, with a few more moving parts and complications than you might find in a "normal" sale, if there is such a thing.

I cold called the offices of other surgeons starting with the nearest communities, and quickly found a couple of doctors open to a second location. I explained that time was of the essence. One of the doctors and his associate wanted to go forward. Ironically, the new buyer's attorney was the same one that Kathy had just released. So the buyer's attorney was fully up to speed with the seller's scenario, but there was a real legal concern: How can an attorney represent the buyer when he formerly represented the seller and is privy to the seller's confidential information? Given that the attorney cannot forget what he knows, can we do all this correctly.

Bottom line: We figured it out, and we closed the deal on the last day of the year. I had known Kathy for only two weeks.

BOOK JOE HRUBAN
TO SPEAK

Book Joe Hruban as your Speaker and you're guaranteed to make your next event, association meeting, or study club highly informative, engaging, and memorable.

Over the years, Joe Hruban has been educating, entertaining, motivating and inspiring practice owners as their career paths transition from active practice to the next chapter in their lives.

Joe can share relevant, actionable positioning strategies and concepts which practice owners can use to better serve their clients and patients.

His unique style will give your group a perspective which will inspire them to think differently and open their minds to using tools and strategies to further design, grow, and transition from active practice whether they are 1 or 9 years from the final steps in their exit plan.

For more information and to book Joe for your next event, visit

www.DVM-Transitions.com/Speaking or call or text (530) 746-8839.

APPENDIX :

Check List – Five Years Before Your Exit

☑	**Get written agreements with associates in place (assignable, non-competes)**
☑	**Consider a consultant to help you get growth in revenues and profits.**
☑	**Consider getting a valuation or appraisal done, sets a benchmark level. (Does not have to be a "full blown" $6,000 appraisal.) For a complimentary "Snapshot Valuation" visit: www.DVM-Transitions.com/Snapshot**
☑	**Make a 5 year plan with goals and milestones based on your values**
☑	**Take care of any EPA risks (chemicals, wastes, etc.)**

APPENDIX :

Check List - Two to Three Years
Before Your Target Exit

☑	Review your personal financial position for life after the sale.
☑	Position yourself so you can afford to retire
☑	Consider practice upgrades (imaging, software, etc.)
☑	Practice consultant engaged? If not, this may be the time.
☑	What responsibilities can be delegated to the team? Systematized checklists?
☑	Is there an emergency referral relationship in place for after hours calls?
☑	Are there equipment leases in place? If so, review terms for early pay downs.
☑	If the Real Estate is not owned, is the lease transferable? When is the next renewal? Visit: www.DVM-Transitions.com/RealEstate

APPENDIX :

Check List – Final Year Before
Your Target Exit

☑	Prepare inventory and equipment lists
☑	Enhance the cosmetic appearance, paint, landscape, repairs etc.
☑	Compile practice information for buyer's review – financial statements, HR records, other agreements etc.
☑	Facility and Real Estate matters, if owned consider the pro and cons of keeping the property vs selling the property. Visit: www.DVM-Transitions.com/RealEstate

ABOUT THE AUTHOR

Joseph Hruban is a seasoned leader in advising doctors and brokering veterinary practice transactions.

With a consultative approach, and a broad business background spanning from his early years on Wall Street to the unique challenges of the veterinary profession today, Joe brings on his clients' behalf over thirty years of hands-on and people-smart deal-making and trusted negotiating experience.

Though he sat for the CPA exam, and has a degree in accounting, Joe has never been an accountant. With deep experience in combining the science of financial matters with the art of dealing with people, Joe is uniquely qualified and positioned to help clients plan for and execute their eventual transitions.

Joe's mission is to help doctors anticipate and navigate through the myriad interwoven complexities of life events and practice transitions. Whether you are an old timer or a newer practitioner, his approach is highly focused and firmly anchored to your unique personal needs & requirements.

From finding and matching buyers for the practice owner, to handling negotiations and getting the deal to the finish line, Joe Hruban is passionate about helping his clients get the best possible transition solution.

Joe is a frequent speaker at veterinary conferences and private industry functions. He and Debbie live in Davis, California with their two dogs, and they always make sure to block off time to discover out-of-the-way places for hiking, skiing, fishing, paddling and camping.

You can reach Joe at joe@dvm-transitions.com or by phone at 530-746-8839 (voice or text).